Praise for Good Trouble

"To heal America's broken heart, we must offer a new American narrative. In a time of great awakening, Noxon takes us on a soul journey that is equal parts painful and promising. This is a story of faith, song, and love . . . the cornerstones of social change. This book is a treasure."

— Rabbi Sharon Brous

"Christopher Noxon's elegant sketches and visceral use of words brilliantly capture the urgent courage and integrity required of the men and women who stepped up for the civil rights movement. Noxon's personal and emotional storytelling walks us right into the story so that, as each page goes by, we begin to see not a history lesson but instead feel a riveting call to action for our own present day. At this moment in time, when leadership feels like it's on life support and we are all aching for something to believe in, *Good Trouble* is not just good medicine—it's the best medicine."

— Shonda Rhimes

"Christopher writes and paints directly from the heart, holding nothing back, thank goodness. These words and drawings make me feel as if I'm on the journey, from the fifties to the present day, from political desperation to hope at the mountain top. *Good Trouble* is a vibrant, much needed reflection on the past and present of civil rights in America and should be required reading for all."

—**Wendy MacNaughton**, author of *Meanwhile in San Francisco*

"*Good Trouble* is an astonishing accomplishment, a history of not just the struggle for justice and civil rights in this country but the moral, spiritual, and even musical underpinnings to those struggles—all told with a fierce economy of words and dozens of seemingly casual but clearly carefully considered illustrations. The drawings, like the title of this book, embody some of the great and wonderful contradictions of the civil rights movement: less is more, deep insight isn't always wordy, and outrage isn't action."

—**Robert F. Darden**, author of *Nothing but Love in God's Water*

"The combination of text and artwork connect us to characters in this riveting narrative in an entirely new way. *Good Trouble* will become a classic in the literature of social movements and nonviolence. Like Jean Merrill's groundbreaking *The Pushcart War* and the classic comic *Martin Luther King and the Montgomery Story*, this book gives readers an emotionally and intellectually deep introduction to core principles of social movements, nonviolence, and the civil rights movement."

—**Paul Engler**, cofounder of activist training institute Momentum, and coauthor of *This Is an Uprising: How Nonviolent Revolt Is Shaping the Twenty-First Century*

GOOD TROUBLE

LESSONS FROM THE CIVIL RIGHTS PLAYBOOK

Christopher Noxon

Abrams, New York

Foreword

The book you hold does not romanticize the Freedom Struggle. Instead, Christopher Noxon does something far more valuable for our evolving American story. He colors history between the cracks of serendipity, spiritual encounters, and Black religiosity. To quote an elder from my community, Noxon places us between "Oh, Lord" and "Thank you, Jesus" of the Freedom Struggle.

This book, I believe, captures the spiritual gumbo of the holy mischief practiced by activist Fanny Lou Hamer, the fierce grace uttered by professor James Lawson, and the moral courage of civil rights leader Bayard Rustin. Noxon allows the reader, whether spiritual or not, to appreciate the Africanized faith at the heart of the movement and also its secular side. This is no small achievement. Many scholars have attempted to document the influence of the Freedom Struggle, whether it's upon music, theology, or spiritual inspiration, but ultimately, they fall short because of the academic restrictions placed upon the scholar.

As a writer and illustrator, Noxon allows his imagination, skill, and spirit to mingle with the stories he records to craft a narrative with whimsical and impressionistic illustrations that speak to what the human vocabulary has difficulty articulating: the intersection of history, divine urgency, and moral imagination. I fell in love with this book's combination of art, myth, history, and poetic wonder. I grew up hearing the names, dates, places, and actions recorded by this work, and Noxon gives life in word and picture to what danced in my imagination as a little boy when I heard these stories shared by the lions of the movement.

Our nation needs *Good Trouble*, a book that creates a mythos in the African sense. I do not use the term *mythos* to mean the acts in this publication are untrue; myth for people of African descent is the sharing of an ultimate truth through the power of community story. It is the role of the griot, or wandering poet, to share the national story for the next generation so they can gain wisdom and truth from the ancestors. *Good Trouble* has been written by a reluctant griot, who, unbeknownst to him, has been given a sacred task to shape a story of women and men who dared to disrupt the lie of racial supremacy and offer a new narrative to reshape an emerging democracy called America.

May your reading of this book be blessed, and let it lead to sacred trouble in these "yet-to-be United States of America." Let us all get into some *Good Trouble* together, and maybe a new nation shall be born.

Rev. Dr. Otis Moss III
Senior Pastor
Trinity United Church of Christ
Chicago, Illinois
May 2018

INTRODUCTION

"We need in every community a group of ANGELIC TROUBLEMAKERS. Our power is in our ability to make things UNWORKABLE. The only weapon we have is our BODIES and we need to TUCK THEM IN PLACES so wheels don't turn."

— Bayard Rustin

Two days after the election of Donald Trump, I was in Memphis, running on fumes, on the third stop of a book tour that suddenly felt STUPID and INCONSEQUENTIAL.

I was sleep-deprived and dumbfounded (also raw and exasperated and more than a little terrified).

But there I was, with a free day in a city I'd never visited. I'd planned to visit Graceland, but now the idea of gawking at FAB seventies interiors felt ... gross.

So I took a cab downtown to the National Civil Rights Museum, thinking it would occupy an hour or two. The car pulled up to the listed address, I got out, looked up and ... no museum in sight.

Instead there was a classic sixties roadside split-level motel. It looked familiar ... the patterned railing, the fold of the drapes, the letters in bubbles on the sign above ...

Oh God.

This was the place.

I had no idea.

With no real warning,
in a burst, I came undone.

Sobbing, hard, standing alone on the street
at eleven A.M. on a sunny Thursday morning.

FULL UGLY CRY.

Why?

The election of 2016 didn't feel like a political event. It felt like an asteroid hit, like a dam broke, like a sinkhole swallowed up Main Street. It felt like 9/11, like an absurd apocalyptic nightmare. It felt catastrophic.

The campaign
was bad enough—
that felt awful too, but
that felt like being underwater,
swimming to the surface . . .

Soon we'd pop out, take a deep breath, and all would be well.

Instead the election came and the surface was ice. We're still underwater.

We're stuck down here.

Stuck in a country threatened by hard-right ideologues, corporate superpowers, white supremacists, and grab-'em-by-the-pussy predators. Stuck in a churning boil of outrage and panic. It's easy to suspect that the whole democratic experiment is coming apart before our very eyes.

It's worth stopping here for a moment to acknowledge what a lot of people would say to this sort of reckoning:

NO DUH.

Nothing I felt standing on the street in Memphis will be news to a lot of Americans. What felt apocalyptic to me is understood as an ongoing truth of life in America to many others.

I'm a privileged white guy, and as such I will never truly understand the lived experience of systemic and generational injustice.

Still, I know that honestly confronting and overcoming that oppression will take ALL OF US working together. We're all faced with the same central question:

HOW DO WE GO ON?

After my little breakdown on the street, I headed inside
(the museum is cleverly contained within the Lorraine's facade).

It turned out the National Civil Rights Museum has a lot to
say about our particular historical moment.

It's a story of despair transformed into resolve, of moral
clarity focused against oppression, of a determined coalition
finding new ways to resist an entrenched and
hostile establishment.

The mugshots of civil rights protestors alone: God.

Young and old, black and white. They were taunted, beaten, hosed, humiliated.

They should be angry, fearful, bitter. Maybe they were? Their faces are pictures of calm, clarity, dignity, defiance, poise...

There is so much to learn.

Like a lot of people, I first learned about civil rights in grade school. The story had a lot of moving parts and a big cast of characters, but the essential bits fit into a neat and—as I was to discover—GROSSLY OVERSIMPLIFIED timeline:

1954 Brown v. Board of Education. Supreme Court desegregates schools!

1955 Rosa Parks arrested for refusing to give up her seat on bus. Movement begins!

1957 Little Rock Nine. Stoic kids defy racist thugs!

1960 Lunch counter sit-ins. Brave college students shoved and abused.

1961 Freedom Rides. More abuse and heroism, this time on buses.

1963 March on Washington, MLK's "I Have a Dream" speech.

1963 Church bombing in Birmingham. Four girls die, nation mourns.

1964 LBJ signs Civil Rights Act! (Whites Only signs come down!)

After that, the curriculum moved into the murkier territory of Vietnam and Watergate, civil rights filed away as the MARCH FROM MONTGOMERY TO MEMPHIS, with Dr. King leading the way against a racist old guard before being martyred on a motel balcony.

Civil rights was a story with a beginning, middle, and end; it was a story of a persecuted minority triumphing over a racist establishment.

It was only after my trip to Memphis and subsequent dive into movement history that I began to appreciate the gaps, errors, and misrepresentations I'd picked up along the way.

That standard story is sugarcoated, simplified, and secularized. It ignores huge swaths of history, elevates certain leaders (mostly male ministers) into mythic heroes, and ignores ongoing oppression.

Most egregiously, the timeline is all off. Civil rights didn't begin with Rosa Parks and it didn't end with the Civil Rights Act. The story of oppression and resistance is as old as the country...

...and as current as today's news.

Also, while Dr. King got the headlines and the Nobel Prize (and nine hundred street names!), the truth is that civil rights was a

POPULAR UPRISING

that owes its biggest advances to ordinary people whose names are not widely known today.

More often than not, these men and women LED THE LEADERS.

Fannie Lou Hamer and Ella Baker

Which brings us here, to this.

And what IS this exactly?

It's the account of an anxious American on a civil rights bender.

It's an appreciation of bravery and moral clarity and tactical know-how.

It's a grab bag of the first principles and winning strategies of arguably the most effective citizen-led social movement in US history, a review of the struggle's

BIG IDEAS and hard-won TACTICS.

Here's what it isn't:

THIS IS NOT an excuse for political posturing. I pledge right here to avoid any further mention of the president-who-shall-not-be-named. The lessons of civil rights transcend the particulars of any one political reality; its playbook offers wisdom and practical know-how to anyone challenging unjust power.

THIS IS NOT an authoritative or official account—I don't speak FOR anyone but myself. I'm just a guy with a pen and notebook and (I hope, on good days) an open mind and open heart.

I'm far removed from the events described herein by time and space and race. I'm super self-conscious about that last part—I'm well aware of the long and painful history of white folks co-opting the experience and pain and talents and know-how of African Americans for their own personal gain.*

Jennifer Epps-Addison of the Center for Popular Democracy

* For the record, I'm donating all author proceeds from the sale of this book to the Center for Popular Democracy, a fierce and inspiring activist group that focuses on racial justice, poverty, and health care.

I'm inspired and guided by civil rights legend/US Congressman John Lewis, who insists the movement was NEVER a struggle that pitted black and white against one another. INTEGRATION is more than a legal standard; it's an aspiration, an inspiration, an acceptance of togetherness.

Integration means we stand up for one another; an injury against you is a wound to me; we are all part of what Dr. King called

THE BELOVED COMMUNITY.

Congressman John Lewis and colleagues sitting on the floor of Congress during a gun control debate.

I.e., we all have a part to play.

I.e., "All life is interrelated. We are all caught in an inescapable network of mutuality, tied into a single garment of destiny."
—Martin Luther King Jr.

Yes to that.

Yes to STANDING UP FOR ONE ANOTHER. Yes to MUTUALITY. Yes to INTEGRATION.

More than anything, this is meant to be a call to learn the lessons of the movement, lessons as relevant now as ever in making change for today and all time.

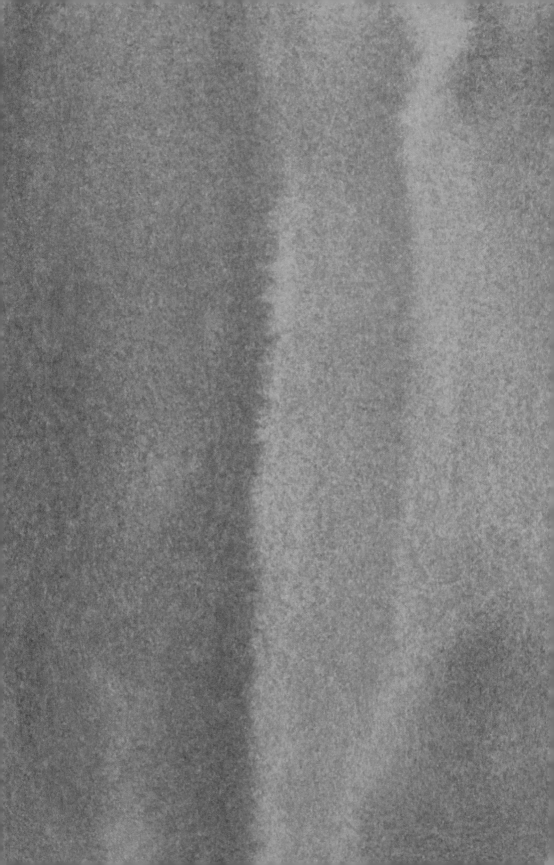

BE BRAVE

FIRST THINGS FIRST: The big advances in civil rights did not result from lawsuits or legislation.

Politics and policy were important, but the movement's momentum flooded over into the everyday world, pushed by ordinary people, propelled through a process known as DIRECT ACTION.

Sit-ins, strikes, Freedom Rides, marches, boycotts, civil disobedience—the movement advanced by putting BODIES IN SPACE, enlisting ordinary people in strategic confrontations with hostile opponents.

As a boy in rural Alabama, John Lewis vividly remembers his mother warning him to guard himself when he'd go into town. Speaking from his congressional office in Washington, DC, Lewis told me how his mother prepared him to deal with a hostile and segregated community. "She'd say, 'Be careful, be watchful, be mindful, and DON'T GET IN TROUBLE.'"

But once Lewis went away to college in Nashville and got active in the movement, he came to see the power of TROUBLE.

"When you see something that is not right, not fair, not just, you have a moral obligation to do something—and in the final analysis, that means you're gonna get into some trouble, necessary trouble, GOOD TROUBLE."

Lewis's phrase has become a rallying cry. Even now, seventy-eight years old and a veteran member of Congress, he is still a big believer in TROUBLEMAKING.

The genius of direct action is how it taps into a natural resource far more powerful than anything the armed, state-sponsored opponents of freedom possess: BRAVERY.

It's hard to even fathom the courage required to act up in an age when activism is so often passive, virtual, and symbolic.

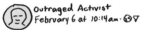

Imagine what it took to join an interstate Freedom Ride or be the first black student at an all-white school or hold your seat at a segregated lunch counter.

These actions were designed to put people in dangerous places. They were meant to ignite and invite DISCOMFORT, SHAME, and even VIOLENCE.

Confrontation, determination, sacrifice, comfort with DISRUPTION—these were the job requirements.

The most significant victories in civil rights were not won as part of orderly policy negotiations—they were forced by activists standing up against oppression.

The lesson:

CHANGE DOES NOT OCCUR IN SAFE SPACES.

Charles Mauldin was fourteen when the movement began in Selma, Alabama. The soft-spoken son of a nurse mom and truck driver dad, Mauldin remembers going to meetings with organizers who asked the students why they couldn't eat at downtown restaurants or use certain drinking fountains.

"We'd been taught never to ask those kinds of questions," he says. "Even asking questions like that could get us killed."

By the time he was sixteen, Mauldin had been arrested three times, beaten with batons, prodded with cattle prods, and made to run miles out of town in a forced march.

"You people like to march so much," said Sheriff Jim Clark. "SO MARCH!"

Mauldin was sixth in line on the first march across the Edmund Pettus Bridge on what came to be known as Bloody Sunday. He remembers kneeling to pray in front of police wielding clubs wrapped in barbed wire. He remembers hiding under the bridge to escape the tear gas.

He remembers running to Brown Chapel, where organizer C. T. Vivian stood on the church steps, standing his ground against a trooper on horseback.

Mauldin tells me all this one rainy morning in Birmingham. He's seventy now, a retired utility worker. The events in Selma were a lifetime ago.

Hearing about his experiences in Selma now, I have to ask: Weren't you TERRIFIED?

"Fear didn't register," he says. "When your consciousness is opened up to a certain point, you don't work out of fear. You're indignant.

YOU ICE YOURSELF from fear."

And sometimes, danger produces something else entirely. It can generate personal transformation.

John Lewis felt something change in him during the lunch counter sit-ins.

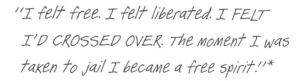

He recalls facing down the hatred of violent segregationists and brutal police with calm resolve.

Hadn't he been afraid? No.

"I felt free. I felt liberated. I FELT I'D CROSSED OVER. The moment I was taken to jail I became a free spirit."*

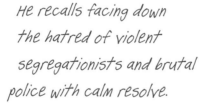

* Lewis is afraid of only two things—lightning and snakes.

Joanne Bland was also there on the bridge on Bloody Sunday. She got involved in the movement early—her first arrest came at the age of eight.

"I wasn't so brave—I was just THERE," she says. "I had no idea what we were doing wasn't normal."

It wasn't normal—news footage of Bland and her fellow protesters being beaten on the Edmund Pettus Bridge was broadcast across the country and around the world, prompting President Lyndon Johnson to declare "we shall overcome" on the floor of the US Congress and leading directly to the Voting Rights Act.

Bland still lives a few miles away from the bridge. One spring day she stands with my eleven-year-old son and a group of his school buddies on a civil rights tour.

"Social movements are jigsaw puzzles!" she says. "And it takes all the pieces to make a complete picture. You are the most important piece!

"Think about the ordinary people who changed not only this little town but America! And then go GET OFF YOUR BEHINDS and do something!"

And remember what she calls the three Ms:

1. **MOTIVATION.** You need to counteract despair and outrage. That's what Dr. King provided more than anything else: INSPIRATION.

2. **MONEY.** No revolution can be fought without funds.

3. **MEDIA.** If no one sees what happens, you're sunk.

Bland's advice leaves the kids feeling inspired, encouraged, and a little scared.

So does all of Selma—especially the Edmund Pettus Bridge.

Crossing over in the footsteps of Bland and Lewis and Mauldin and all the brave souls who made this journey, you expect to feel something EPIC. The full weight of history. Instead, it feels entirely ordinary—and a little creepy.

The bridge is an unlovely steel crossing studded with rivets and named after a grand wizard of the KKK. We're downwind from a monstrous paper mill; the breeze is sour and rotten.

This is a real place, a sad place.

It's a letdown.

Real people and places
are complicated
and sometimes
unpleasant.

Of course they are. Of course WE are.

And maybe the bravery that fueled those ordinary people isn't
so unfathomable after all.

Maybe BRAVERY ISN'T A SUPERPOWER that belongs to only
a select few.

Dorie Ladner was a teenager when she helped start the Student Nonviolent Coordinating Committee (SNCC—pronounced "SNICK"!), the young, idealistic, activist wing of the movement. Along with the Congress of Racial Equality (CORE), it organized some of the most daring, dangerous direct actions.

"We started from the bottom up— meaning that we were DOWN WITH THE PEOPLE, and the people are the leaders in any community. So all we did was listen to the people and help them to act on the things that were bothering them." —Dorie Ladner

Jo Ann Robinson is another unsung hero of the movement— more on her later. For now, here's what she said about the role of ordinary people in making the movement work:

"The amazing thing about our movement is that it's a protest of the people. It's not a one-man show. It's not the preachers' show. It's the people. The masses of this town, who are tired of being trampled on, are responsible. The leaders couldn't stop it if they wanted to."

These ordinary people stood up in bravery and joy and pain and togetherness. They awakened the conscience of the world.

With courage and know-how, they changed laws, opened minds, and inspired generations of activists.

GET ORGANIZED

We all know the story.

Rosa Parks, with her granny glasses and her soulful stare, refusing to leave her seat on the bus. Getting hauled off to jail, prompting outrage, protest, boycotts, and within a year...

The entire civil rights movement.

As origin stories go, it's got everything:

An everyday hero. A courageous act. Great and mysterious forces coming into play.

It's of course a lot more complicated than that. For one thing, civil rights didn't begin with Rosa Parks—the real story goes back a whole lot further...

Booker T. Washington
lobbied Theodore Roosevelt
at the White House

Harriet Tubman,
Underground Railroad
conductor and all-around badass

W. E. B. Du Bois was one of the
abolitionists who formed the NAACP in 1909.

The other thing about the Rosa Parks story? She wasn't the
first black bus passenger to say

NO WAY, I'M NOT MOVING.

Two other women had the SAME
experience on the SAME bus
system in the SAME year—
eighteen-year-old Mary
Louise Smith and
fifteen-year-old
Claudette Colvin
(pictured). Both were
handcuffed and locked
up after refusing to give
up their seats to white
passengers.

When Colvin was carted off, she screamed over and over, "It's my constitutional right to sit here as much as that lady! It's my constitutional right!"

And thirteen years before THAT, Bayard Rustin was arrested for refusing to budge on a segregated bus in Kentucky.*

So why does every schoolkid in America know about Rosa Parks but not about Claudette Colvin or Mary Louise Smith or Bayard Rustin or the streetcar protests?

Colvin was an outspoken, pregnant teenager.

Smith was a poor girl from the country whose dad was a drunk.

Rustin was a gay former Communist.

* Boycotting segregation on public transport actually traces back to 1900, when blacks refused to ride streetcars in twenty-five Southern cities.

Rosa Parks was none of that. She was a secretary at the NAACP, and while her arrest wasn't planned, she was everything her bosses were looking for: she was dignified, middle class, and respectable.

Would the movement have accelerated the way it did with Claudette or Mary Louise or Bayard out front? It's hard to know—I hope so. They all faced the same oppression, and they all deserve to be remembered for their bravery.

Even today some people resent how Rosa became the standard-bearer. One day in Selma I met a woman named Olla Fitts Moore. It always bothered her that Rosa "got all the glory."

"They put her out front just 'cause of what she looked like—that's what the white man did in discriminating against us. That don't seem right. You being pretentious."

It's troubling to think of leaders of the movement treating injustice like SHOWBIZ.

Still, SOMEONE needs to carry the banner, and as much as we'd like to believe social justice crusaders are above base superficialities, Rosa Parks was undoubtedly RIGHT for the role she played—just as Sheriff Jim Clark was just the sort of racist hothead civil rights leaders NEEDED when they chose Selma for their next big action—proving that in movements (just as in show business):

CASTING IS KEY.

But even with Rosa Parks, the boycott instead could have easily fizzled. The Montgomery boycott continued for 381 DAYS, focusing the WORLD's attention and galvanizing a massive wave of resistance.

HOW DID THAT HAPPEN?

Good leadership made a difference (more on that later), but a few other X FACTORS are worth remembering:

Dollars and cents. The boycott was ECONOMIC.
It hurt local businesses and hobbled the city bus service.

That became a huge part of the movement going forward—from actions at lunch counters, theaters, and even ice-skating rinks, protest worked best when it affected THE BOTTOM LINE.

"We'd been trying to win over the hearts and minds of Southerners—that was a mistake. We realized in Montgomery you had to hit them in the pocketbook."
—Wyatt Tee Walker

Less obviously, the boycott succeeded because of an innovation unknown in 1955:

Ridesharing.

Like Uber or Lyft? Pretty much, yeah.

A carpool program created during the boycott ran a lot like current ridesharing systems. Without it, the boycott never would have worked.

FORTY THOUSAND PEOPLE needed an alternative to the buses when the boycott began.

Many walked, a few took bikes, some hitchhiked, a few rode mules or traveled in horse-drawn buggies.

But most people had no good options. What to do?

The problem fell to Rufus A. Lewis, director of the town's biggest black funeral parlor. He got the job for a simple reason:

"I had access to cars."

Lewis assembled a fleet of so-called "rolling churches"— within three weeks he had three hundred hearses, taxis, loaned cars,

and station wagons purchased with funds donated by supporters around the country.

Volunteer drivers DASHED around Montgomery, picking up and dropping off people at designated spots near workplaces and schools and transferring riders at a "transportation center" in a downtown parking lot.

THE E.L POSEY
PARKING LOT

I visit the spot where the parking lot used to be on a warm Sunday morning. It's now a park, across the street from the headquarters of Chick-fil-A.

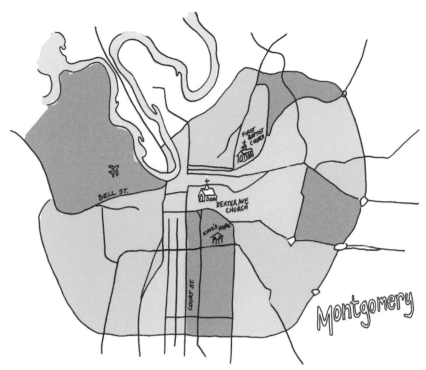

Montgomery

"People would call in, say, 'I'm out here on Cloverdale Road in such-a-such a block, and I'll be ready at such-and-such a time.' This was being done all through the day. We'd bring them to the center, then all those people who lived in North Montgomery would get into a car and be carried to their place."
—Rufus A. Lewis

At its height, the rideshare program made twenty thousand TRIPS A DAY.

Police were dispatched to
pull over anyone suspected of carpooling.

One driver got thirty tickets in two months.

Others (including Rosa Parks, who helped run the dispatch)
were arrested on charges of "conspiring to destroy the
bus company."

City officials went so far as to pressure insurance carriers to cancel coverage of carpool drivers. It's some measure of the boycott's sophistication that they found a backup policy covering the entire carpool with ————————→

LLOYD'S of LONDON.

There's another crucial, predictably forgotten part of the story: WOMEN.

Dr. King is most often portrayed as the star player of the boycott ... but it was in fact instigated, conceived, and maintained by women.

On the day of her arrest, Rosa Parks was discouraged from pursuing the case by her husband, Raymond, who told her:

—— *"The white folks will* ___KILL___ *you!"*

She went ahead anyway.

Late that same night, an English professor at Alabama State College named Jo Ann Robinson called together a group of women. They stayed up all night— Robinson had tried and failed to organize a city bus boycott before, but now she saw her chance.

She drafted the original call for a boycott, and her gang of activist women secretly mimeographed leaflets on university machines and passed them around the city in the morning.

So sure, Rosa Parks got the movement going in a whole new way. The boycott she inspired desegregated the bus system, striking a major blow against Jim Crow laws in the South.

But there's a popular image of Mrs. Parks as an unprepared civilian who rose to mythic heights one day when her feet hurt. In fact, she was a trained activist among many who'd committed themselves to fighting for equality.

And the spark she lit never would've caught without leaders like Martin and planners like Rufus and organizers like Jo Ann.

BE BOLD

After the success of the bus boycott in Montgomery, the movement SPUTTERED and STALLED.

The cautious, respectable ministers at Dr. King's new organization, the Southern Christian Leadership Conference (SCLC), strategized and considered.

Meanwhile, the legal and political minds of the movement in the NAACP weighed the merits of lawsuits and lobbying. School desegregation ran up against stubborn governors, angry mobs, and intractable communities.

The struggle was at a standstill.

KEEP ALABAMA WHITE

THEN CAME
THE SIT-INS.

The sit-ins were the work
of idealistic students impatient
with the slow pace of change.

Joan Trumpauer Mulholland was among a group of students
who sat in at the Woolworth lunch counter in downtown
Jackson, Mississippi, in May of 1963. The group was beaten,
berated, and smeared with condiments—that's Mulholland's
head getting doused with sugar in a picture that became an
iconic image of the movement.

"We could very well
have been killed."

Mulholland was the great-granddaughter of Georgia slave-holders, and her involvement was seen as scandalous and possibly INSANE—she was taken in for psychiatric testing after her first arrest.

Now seventy-six and living in suburban Virginia, Mulholland says she was never all that bothered by fear.

"I don't really DO fear. It's counterproductive. It keeps you from doing what you need to. At the time, I really felt like I went into an out-of-body experience. My body was in a shell—the rest of me was UP ABOVE like a guardian angel."

Beyond developing supernatural
powers of disassociation, she has two
other tips for would-be agitators:

1. **BACKUP IS KEY.** "You never
want to be by yourself. We
always went into one
of these actions with a
SPOTTER or a witness. You
need someone nearby who
doesn't look like they're
involved who can see what's
happening and call the lawyers
if need be."

2. **PRAISE THE PRESS.** Mulholland credits the newspaper
photographer who covered the sit-in with as much heroism as
anyone involved. He kept snapping while being pummeled with
flying debris—other journalists were knocked
to the ground and their cameras were broken.

In an age when distrust and suspicion of the media is rampant, Mulholland says activists should remember:

"The demonstrators take it to the street.

And the lawyers take it to the court, but

THE PRESS TAKE IT TO THE WORLD."

After the sit-ins, Mulholland joined up with students planning an even BOLDER and more DISRUPTIVE act of civil disobedience: THE FREEDOM RIDES.

Begun in the summer of '61, the rides took integrated groups into deeply racist backwaters, testing federal court rulings that banned segregation. The first ride of thirteen provoked mob attacks and left a bus firebombed outside Anniston, Alabama.

Catherine Burks-Brooks was a student at Tennessee A&I at the time. During a Sunday picnic with some activist friends, Burks-Brooks got news that organizers were so alarmed by the firebombing that they'd called off the operation. The group decided to take up the ride themselves.

Burks-Brooks had been bucking up against injustice as long as she could remember. As a girl on her way to school, she hated how white people expected her to move away when they passed. "I resented that. I didn't step aside. If white people crossed me, we bumped.

"I BEEN BUMPING WHITE FOLKS FOR A LONG TIME."

Burks-Brooks's group was picked up outside Birmingham and taken into "protective custody," then left on the side of the road deep in

klan country. They managed to find their way back to Birmingham and get back on the bus, but they ran into more trouble in Montgomery, set upon by another mob that came at them with sticks and bricks.

They spent the night at the First Baptist Church, besieged by a crowd of torch-carrying locals. Federal troops were called in to prevent a massacre.

After rejoining the ride in Mississippi, Burks-Brooks was arrested and sent to Parchman Penitentiary, where she was thrown into a cell next to an electric chair. Her most vivid memory of that experience: the bugs.

"They never stopped swarming."

Together, the sit-ins and the Freedom Rides represented a MAJOR ESCALATION of the movement. The actions were BOLD, DANGEROUS, and POLARIZING. People were forced to TAKE SIDES. Leaders of the movement scrambled to keep up with their followers, pledging support but offering little in the way of material help. When Dr. King told sit-in students he was with them "in spirit," they shot back:

WHERE IS YOUR BODY?

Dr. King took that lesson to heart in early 1963 while planning a major campaign in Birmingham. He and a team of organizers carefully choreographed an operation dubbed PROJECT C—

C for **CONFRONTATION.**

Beginning with a boycott of downtown stores, the campaign continued with smaller sit-ins and marches. When momentum seemed to wane, Dr. King made the controversial decision to be arrested himself.

Dr. King's now-famous LETTER FROM BIRMINGHAM JAIL (written in part on scraps of toilet paper!) was not directed at the brutal cops turning hoses and dogs on protesters. He was more frustrated with the moderates who'd objected to his increasingly disruptive tactics. (Elsewhere, he accused these temperate voices of

"do-nothingism" and "standstillism.")

"Shallow understanding from people of good will is more frustrating than absolute misunderstanding from people of ill will," he wrote. "Lukewarm acceptance is much more bewildering than outright rejection."

The BOLDEST and potentially most DANGEROUS move of the Birmingham campaign was the so-called CHILDREN'S CRUSADE. The crusade sent schoolkids, some as young as six years old, onto the streets. On the first day, five hundred arrests were made. More came a day later, and still more the next day, with more than a THOUSAND kids rounded up and jailed in makeshift detention centers around the city on one day alone.

City officials buckled under the public pressure, agreeing to take down Whites Only signs and integrate hiring at downtown establishments. Just as they had made a crucial difference in the sit-ins, KIDS CREATED CHANGE in Birmingham. Dr. King's tactic had been proved:

PRESSURE IS FAR MORE EFFECTIVE THAN POLICY.

Of course there are downsides and difficulties with such BOLD CONFRONTATIONAL tactics.

For one thing, BACKLASHES are inevitable. Newton's third law applies: For every action there is an equal and opposite reaction. Abe Lincoln was murdered during the emancipation of slaves. The rise of civil rights prompted the rise of Strom Thurmond, who put the segregationist Southern strategy simply:

We will FIGHT to the DEATH!

Dr. King was called a radical communist and an enemy of the state.

Civil rights leaders were labeled as pushy extremists and uncompromising troublemakers. They weren't set back by these reactions; they took them as a POINT OF PRIDE.

They learned another thing as well: DISRUPTION ALONE is no good if it isn't backed with specific demands and ongoing organization.

THE LESSON: Dramatic actions can force adversaries to the table, but lasting change happens with deliberate and ongoing negotiation.

STILL, as the sit-ins, Freedom Rides, and events in Birmingham make clear, a movement needs YOUTH and BOLD ACTS OF COURAGE.

HAVE FAITH

Can I get an amen?

Can I get a hallelujah?

The time has come, friends, for church.

Any honest attempt to understand civil rights has got to reckon with FAITH and GOD and the role of RELIGION.

It's a subject many today would rather avoid, mostly because such talk has been dominated for so long by fundamentalists less interested in civil rights and social justice than issues like abortion, gay marriage, or prayer in schools.

It's hard to remember a time when conservatives didn't dominate discussion of religion and politics.

But it hasn't always been this way. Religion was undoubtedly a FORCE FOR PROGRESS AND FREEDOM during the civil rights movement, transcending politics and drawing power from the DEEP SPIRITUAL TRADITIONS and GRASSROOTS ORGANIZATION of the church. And to many (most?) of the people on the front lines of the movement, faith was at the center of the story.

"The protest ... cannot be explained without a divine dimension. ... **Some extra-human force** labors to create a harmony out of the discords of the universe."
—Martin Luther King Jr.

WHATEVER OUR BELIEFS ABOUT THAT EXTRA-HUMAN FORCE, it's worth asking: How DID faith serve the movement? And can't we summon some of that same power back to the side of social justice?

The first thing to recognize: Religion wasn't exclusive to any denomination or even one faith. Born in the Baptist church, civil rights was inspired by Hindus (Gandhi) and transcendentalists (Henry David Thoreau). It was supported by a far-flung network of Jews, Quakers, Catholics, and people of pretty much all religious backgrounds.

The movement also included the nonreligious—A. Philip Randolph, the union chief and civil rights leader who helped desegregate the military, was an atheist.

All of which is to say: THE MORE THE MERRIER. Making room for religion in social action means converting to what Rev. Dr. Katharine Henderson calls a "multifaith perspective."

Henderson grew up in Kentucky; her parents were active in the movement. Tagging along with her parents as a little girl to civil rights marches and church meetings made a big impression:

"I learned the muscle memory of PRAYING WITH YOUR FEET.*"

* How good is that phrase? All credit and reverence to Abraham Heschel, the Jewish scholar and author.

"The fusion of streets and pew—that's in my DNA. It gets SPARKED and QUICKENED every time I'm out there at a protest. It's where I feel the spirit of God at work in the world."

Henderson is president of the Auburn Seminary, a crack team of religious leaders of all faiths who draw on the lessons of civil rights to fight for social justice. She tells me all about it one summer afternoon in her New York office, describing the birth of the NEW RELIGIOUS LEFT.

The powerhouse group includes Rev. William Barber (heir to Dr. King and head of a revived Poor People's Campaign) and Rabbi Sharon Brous (prophetic LA rabbi who rocked the Women's March on Washington). They're like progressive superheroes.

Unlike the relatively coherent coalition of Christian conservatives (read: Protestant, white), this group is diverse and often disjointed. Henderson says there's a trick to making it work:

"You lean deeply into the particularity of your own religious tradition—but you GIVE UP THE SUPERIORITY."

They all agree on a central shared notion that can be boiled down into two words:

SOUL FORCE.

That's one translation for the sanskrit word SATYAGRAHA, coined by Gandhi and taken up by Dr. King to describe the fierce, universal, nonviolent, openhearted, deeply rooted RESOLVE that animated both the Indian independence movement and civil rights.

SOUL FORCE is about summoning a higher power* in confronting injustice.

* Here's Dr. King again with a better description: "There is a creative personal power in this universe who is the ground and essence of all reality."

I get a crash course in SOUL FORCE one Sunday morning in a central LA church with Dr. James Lawson, guiding spirit and a leading figure of the movement.

Dr. Lawson created a "nonviolent laboratory" in Nashville, Tennessee, to train activists—

including John Lewis and Diane Nash. In newsreel footage, he's the tweedy academic at the blackboard, explaining how SOUL FORCE worked in Biblical battles, colonial India, and France under Nazi occupation.

John Lewis recalls huddling in a classroom every weeknight for an entire school year before ever stepping into a protest.

"People think that we woke up one morning and said we're going to protest. No. We planned, we studied, we organized. We were preparing ourselves. It's a discipline."

Lawson is eighty-nine now, but he's lost none of his urgency. People mistakenly think of the nonviolent philosophy as passive, he says. They think it's sanctimonious, nonconfrontational, avoidant, a submissive capitulation to the will of the powerful.

It's NONE of those things.

"It's love in action. It's ENERGY and POWER. It takes DISCIPLINE and VIGILANCE."

SOUL FORCE is direct, strategic, and spiritual. It's not about shying away from a fight. It's about confronting opposition head-on, breaking the cycle of aggression and retribution that rewards power over humanity, might over right, and belligerence over wisdom.

After the assassinations of Dr. King and Malcolm X and the rise of Black Power, many in the movement changed their tune about nonviolence. Not Dr. Lawson. He believes SATYAGRAHA is more important now than ever.

"The mythology of violence and war is dominant in the United States—we live in a plantation economy that exalts individualism and SMOTHERS the miraculous, spectacular, and astonishing gift of life."

"AMEN TO THAT," calls Otis Moss III, Chicago pastor, son of movement veterans, and current-day civil rights warrior.* Too many people today, he says, equate religion with dogma and forget how faith can ELEVATE and ENLIGHTEN the work of social justice.

"We've taken God out of the civil rights story," he says. "This wasn't just black people singing songs and saying 'help me Jesus.' There's a deep spiritual ethic at work, an ancient black tradition that goes back to West Africa and that continues right up to current-day readings of the Bible.

"We see this play out in our lives. The Bible literally matches our reality."

* He's also, delightfully, a huge comics nerd! So much so that he assigned all his fellow Auburn Seminary fellows Justice League alter egos!

Maybe it's pure sociology—maybe civil rights was born in the black church because that's where people (particularly women) got organized. Or maybe GOD HAD A DIRECT HAND in guiding this momentous shift in American history.

Who knows? I toggle between skepticism and faith, but I admit:

I'm definitely ROOTING for the God squad.

And every once in a while something happens that makes it feel like there's definitely an EXTRA-HUMAN FORCE at work. Like a miraculous experience I had one summer morning at LaGuardia Airport.

Some background: I'd spent three months holed up at the Schomburg Center for Research in Black Culture in Harlem reading up on the movement and its history.

I wanted to meet and interview and draw people who'd been involved—but had little luck arranging meetings. Phone calls went unreturned. Emails were ignored. I started to despair. I had no real standing in their world. However sympathetic I might feel in this moment, I feared I was viewed as just another clueless observer looking for a quick hit of understanding.

Still, I took a cue from the movement: PUT BODIES IN SPACE. Go to the places where the movement played out, walk the streets, meet people face-to-face. I booked a ticket to Atlanta and hoped for the best (while expecting the worst).

So there I am waiting to take off on my Southern field trip, wedged into the corner of a ridiculously crowded Southwest terminal.

Through the crowd comes a dapper gentleman in a white fedora.

His guide dog sniffs and heads toward my corner. I move around some luggage to make room.

Whereupon a woman sitting a few feet away drops an enormous cup of iced coffee on the floor. It explodes on impact, splattering our pant legs, our bags, and the dog, who starts lapping up the coffee excitedly.

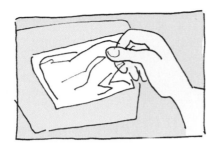

Oh no! I help pull the dog away, then run over to a concession stand and grab a wad of napkins.

Doing my best to wipe up the spill and dry off the dog, I get to talking with the man in the spiffy hat. He tells me how glad he is that his dog, Kelly, didn't lap up too much coffee before the flight.

We do that thing you do at airports where you ask if you're on your way home or headed on a trip.

He's headed home. To Montgomery, Alabama. To a house a mile or two away from Dexter Avenue Church, you know, where Dr. King started the Montgomery bus boycott?

He lives there with his wife, Avis, whom he met while giving tours of important sites in civil rights history. He was pastor at Dexter a few years ago.

Pleased to meet you, Rev. R. K. Smith.

This is altogether MIRACULOUS, no? EXTRA-HUMAN, even?

R. K. and I have a lot to talk about. He tells me about losing his sight from glaucoma. About his mentor, Dr. Bernard Lafayette, one of Dr. King's inner circle. About his wife growing up at Dexter Avenue Church with King and his family. I tell Rev. R. K. about my three kids and my experience in Memphis and what I'm working on and HOW FLABBERGASTING our meeting like this feels. (He says simply, "God has a plan for us.")

In Montgomery
I join him for
Sunday service at
Dexter. He takes
me to his favorite
barbecue joint.

We go with Miss Avis on a tour of the town,
past the Confederate statues and
movement meeting places, stopping
for oysters on the banks of the
Alabama River and soul food by
the highway. We sit on his front
porch and sample 'Bama hooch.

Mrs.B's! →

The Alabama
Confederate
Monument is
eighty-eight
feet tall!

I despair at the state of the country, the rise of white nationalists, and the insanity of our politics. But R. K. isn't having it: He's unfailingly upbeat.

"It's a GREAT time to be alive," he says. "Where would we be without struggle? What's happening now is nothing. You wanna talk about bleak? Let's talk about how my ancestors survived, through displacement and slavery and the Civil War and lynchings and Jim Crow. THESE IDIOTS IN CHARGE TODAY ARE LIGHTWEIGHTS."

"And now we got all kinds of good people standing up against evil—black folks and white folks, Latinos and Asians and gays, everyone standing up and fighting."

We got work to do, and we're doing it — TOGETHER."

BE NONVIOLENT

Rev R. K. Smith's wife, Avis Dunbar, remembers the night Dr. King's house was bombed. She lived just down the street—the explosion rattled her windows. She was five years old.

A crowd gathered around the front porch.

"People were out with hammers and guns," she remembers. "They were mad. They were ready to fight."

She remembers watching Dr. King venture outside. She knew him from church. Standing in the January chill, Dr. King reassured everyone that he, Coretta, and their baby girl were unhurt. He told everyone to go home and put away their weapons. There would be no retaliation—they would not answer violence with violence.

"This is not our way," he said.

NOT OUR WAY.

The story of civil rights is deeply rooted in Dr. King's words on that bombed-out porch. As both a philosophy and a tactic, NONVIOLENCE WAS THE GUIDING PRINCIPLE, THE PRIMARY TACTIC,

THE BEATING HEART OF THE MOVEMENT.

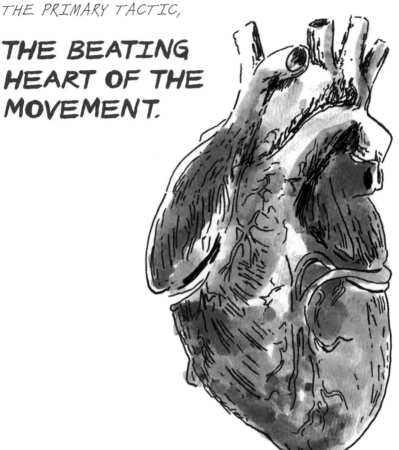

The movement wasn't ALL peace and love and forgiveness. Many more activists and organizers and ordinary citizens carried weapons and fought back than is commonly recognized.

In Monroe, North Carolina, a former Marine named Robert Williams led a group called the BLACK GUARD to fight segregationist terrorism with "armed self-reliance."

In Louisiana, a group of veterans acted as armed security for voter registration activists and vulnerable citizens under the banner DEACONS FOR DEFENSE AND JUSTICE.

But the greatest gains of the movement—the new legal protections, the dismantling of Jim Crow, the radical change in public sympathies—did not result from acts of armed self-defense.

Progress was made through a kind of SPIRITUAL JUJITSU—turning acts of aggression against the aggressor.

The more they strike, the more you win.

"The civil rights movement has no greater friend than its enemy. It is the enemy of civil rights who again and again produces the evidence that we cannot afford to stand still."
—Rep. Emanuel Celler, chair of House Judiciary Committee

Dr. King understood that—and that made him "the BADDEST CAT WALKING THE BLOCK."

So says Dr. Clarence Jones, Dr. King's lawyer and friend. At eighty-seven, he's one of the last surviving members of Dr. King's inner circle. (He helped draft the "I Have a Dream" speech!) We talked strategy and philosophy one lovely October evening under a starry California sky.

"Do you know what the genius of Martin Luther King was? Why nonviolent resistance was and is such an effective tool? You want to know why?"

Yes I do, Dr. Jones. I SO want to know.

"Those who want to continue the worst policies of the past WANT you to be violent. We give them a gift when we engage in violence. Then all anyone pays attention to is THAT and NOT our underlying message. Dr. King understood that. That's why the dude was so powerful!"

As a strategy, Dr. Jones says, nonviolence is fragile. It requires unanimity. In a march of thousands of people, a few hotheads swinging punches or breaking windows will WRECK AND UNDERMINE an entire cause and put everyone at risk.

Which is why it's crucial for activists to SELF-POLICE against agitators (who are sometimes covert operators— provocateurs!—secretly working for the other side to incite violence. This happened ALL THE TIME in civil rights demonstrations). More than two thousand deputies worked the crowd at the 1963 National March on Washington for Jobs and Freedom to stop skirmishes.

So, lesson time: NONVIOLENCE IS ACTIVE. IT REQUIRES TRAINING AND DISCIPLINE AND SELF-POLICING.

Militants ready to RUMBLE are usually pacified when reminded of an obvious point: On an entirely practical level, violence is counterproductive when one side has the arms and authority.

Outgunned, outnumbered, and unrepresented in government and law enforcement, African Americans would have been DECIMATED in a conventional war.

The same is true today for all marginalized people. When the other side has the guns, it's best not to start a firefight.

Or as economist and activist Michael Albert is quoted as saying in the book THIS IS AN UPRISING:* "A contest of escalating violence is a contest we are DOOMED TO LOSE. A contest in which numbers, commitment, and increasingly militant nonviolent activism confronts state power is a contest we can win."

* Which has a TON of great information on how social movements work— see reading list on page 190.

It really comes down to results. Nonviolent protests are simply more effective—they bring out more people and achieve more objectives than violent rebellions.

In a study of more than three hundred cases of resistance from 1900 to 2006, social scientists Erica Chenoweth and Maria J. Stephan showed that nonviolent campaigns are about ELEVEN TIMES LARGER than violent ones.

Still, nonviolence is not without TROUBLING LIMITS and RAMIFICATIONS.

For one thing, there are nagging questions of SELF-DEFENSE and PRIVILEGE. It's easy for the well-off and safely secured to espouse the absolute primacy of nonviolence. It's a different thing entirely for those under attack.

As movement activist Anne Braden put it:

"I don't think anybody sitting in a safe, comfortable apartment in New York has any right to tell you not to arm yourself."

Another thing that's hard to wrap your head around when it comes to nonviolence: the strategic value of SUFFERING.

If the point of traditional combat is to inflict suffering on your opponent, the point of nonviolent direct action is to ABSORB suffering and expose the aggressor to the light of conscience (and bad publicity).

James Zwerg was attacked at a Montgomery bus station during the Freedom Rides.

Inspired by Gandhi's philosophy of ascetic renunciation
(tapasya) and the Christian belief in the redemptive suffering
of Jesus, suffering occupies an uncomfortable central
place in the nonviolent playbook.
Indeed, civil rights leaders
COURTED and INVITED
and ORCHESTRATED
suffering.

After fourteen-year-old Emmett Till was murdered while visiting relatives
in Mississippi in 1955, his mother Mamie insisted his casket remain open. She
allowed photographs to be published of her son's mutilated body: "People
had to face my son...also people had to face themselves."

Here's Bayard Rustin in his book *Strategies for Freedom*.

"In a situation where the objectives of the social movement are accepted by the majority, protest becomes an effective tactic TO THE DEGREE THAT IT ELICITS BRUTALITY AND OPPRESSION from the power structure. . . . It was not the civil rights movement's program which aroused the conscience of the nation, but the sight of small children entering a Little Rock high school accompanied by a federal troop escort that could not protect them from the jeering cadences of an ugly and irrational mob. Negroes gained moral authority not because Americans opposed segregation, but because black people were suffering, because churches were bombed and children firehosed."

In other words, leaders could TALK TALK TALK about unjust laws and proposed reforms. But what made a difference was when America WITNESSED oppression and suffering for themselves. (Another key point: TV news was a new thing; every night viewers were confronted with same-day footage of Southern brutality.)

Here's how Harry McPherson, President Johnson's speech-writer, put it:

"King's suffering was the catalyst. His being beaten, his being hosed, his being put in jail, all of the suffering that he endured, in every case, brought a LEGISLATIVE RESPONSE."

The murder of Unitarian minister James Reeb (left) was national news and was instrumental in the passage of the Voting Rights Act. His death came a few weeks after the killing of civil rights activist Jimmie Lee Jackson (right), whose death prompted the Selma to Montgomery march.

No doubt this strategy WORKED. It continues to inspire and inform activists today.

But it also can't be adopted wholesale without honest soul-searching. It was one thing for civil rights activists to expose segregationists in the Deep South ... it's another for activists fighting today. The point should NEVER be to INCITE brutality or CULTIVATE VICTIMHOOD or engage in that tiresome liberal game of OPPRESSION OLYMPICS.

THE POINT IS THIS: The movement didn't get stuck in suffering. Suffering was just the start of the story. It was the flash point, the activating agent, the spark that lit a larger fire.

Suffering ISN'T A SOURCE OF POWER. It isn't even our individual strength.

Activists Michael Schwerner, James Chaney, and Andrew Goodman were murdered by Klansmen on a Mississippi backroad in 1964.

Our power is in our TOGETHERNESS. It's in our recognition of our common humanity. Or as Dr. King put it:

"I can only close the gap in broken community by meeting hate with love.... In the final analysis... all life is interrelated. All humanity is involved in a single process, and all men are brothers.... When I am commanded to love, I am commanded to restore community, to resist injustice, and to meet the needs of my brothers."

LEAD!

In 1955, Martin Luther King was a boyish, hypereducated but heretofore unknown twenty-six-year-old.

Less than a year after his arrival at Dexter Avenue Church, Rosa Parks got arrested on a downtown bus. The community sprang into action, naming King as their leader—partly because he was a young newcomer with less to lose than the established ministers in town.

The timing of that is kind of MIRACULOUS, no?

That's how it felt to Dr. King's followers.

Obvious lesson, one that today's consensus-oriented lefty organizations would do well to remember:

Leadership matters.

And when it comes to leadership, Dr. King had some stellar company. The standard narrative narrows the main players to a group known as the BIG SIX:

(Left to right) John Lewis, SNCC;
Whitney Young, NUL; A. Philip Randolph, BPSC; Martin Luther King Jr., SCLC; James Farmer, CORE; Roy Wilkins, NAACP

These are the famed FATHERS OF THE MOVEMENT.

No doubt these guys deserve a ton of credit—as statesmen, activists, negotiators, shot-callers, and intermediaries between oppressed peoples and a hostile white establishment.

All due respect.

Still—a couple of things to keep in mind about this team at the top:

First, it's worth remembering that the BIG SIX were far from unified. They disagreed with one another ALL THE TIME. There were FIERCE BRAWLS over nonviolence, the role of whites, and compromises in civil rights legislation.

John Lewis, for one, viewed the Civil Rights Act of 1964 as woefully insufficient—his speech at the National March railed against the government and declared the movement a "serious social revolution," worrying moderates.

But when push came to shove, they closed ranks, forming an accountable BLOC devoted to a common cause.

This helped in big ways and small—it gave the movement political capital, and it allowed for informal alliances and support.

One great example: When the super-expensive, state-of-the-art sound system acquired for the March was SABOTAGED the day before the event, organizers made a back-channel call to Attorney General Robert Kennedy for help.

Within hours, the Army Signal Corps was dispatched to rebuild the system, saving the day.

Talk about the benefits of friends in high places.

Lesson: Opposing authority sometimes means working with it.

Don't get carried away with antiestablishment fervor.
INSIDERS AREN'T ALWAYS THE ENEMY.

Another obvious issue with the Big Six: WHERE ARE
THE WOMEN?

What was true during the Montgomery bus strike was true
for the whole movement—while the Big Six were busy
negotiating deals and playing politics, legions of
lesser-known activists, mostly women,
were doing what legendary
behind-the-scenes leader
Ella Baker called
SPADE WORK,
tilling the soil of
the grass roots.

Baker had been fighting for workers and the poor since the 1930s—she came into the movement as an elder organizer with a long resume and big ideas. She didn't like how the black church was set up, with its largely female membership and male leadership.

She pushed for a more inclusive, cooperative approach—at the establishment of the SNCC, she urged students to forge their own path and speak for themselves.

"You didn't see me on television, you didn't see news stories about me. The kind of role that I tried to play was to pick up pieces or put together pieces out of which I hoped organization might come." —Ella Baker

Then there's Fannie Lou Hamer, who's got to be the most inspiring, ferocious, heroic, before-her-time figure in the movement.

Hamer is known for her part in the 1964 Democratic National Convention. As a spokesperson for the new, integrated Mississippi Freedom Democratic Party, she recounted growing up on the Mississippi Delta as the youngest of twenty children (!!) and being beaten nearly to death in jail after registering neighbors to vote.

"I'm SICK and TIRED of being SICK and TIRED."

She was a leader like no other—she walked with a limp, fearlessly poked fun at bigots, and lived with her husband, Pap, in a house with no hot water and no indoor toilet. And her most lasting legacy went far beyond politics.

To Hamer, the key to gaining equality wasn't political at all—it was AGRICULTURAL. With help from Harry Belafonte and a Wisconsin charity, she purchased sixty acres of land in the Delta long dominated by slaveholders and sharecroppers which she developed into what became the seven-hundred-acre FREEDOM FARM and PIG BANK. She and her neighbors planted peas, collard greens, snap beans, cucumbers, and squash.

"When you've got four hundred quarts of greens and gumbo soup canned for the winter, NOBODY CAN PUSH YOU AROUND OR TELL YOU WHAT TO SAY OR DO."

With Freedom Farm, Hamer took activism into the promised land of CREATING ACTUAL COMMUNITIES. Others in the movement followed this path, FORGOING PROTEST in favor of building co-ops, schools, community kitchens, bookstores, and cultural centers that embodied the high ideals of egalitarianism, integration, and mutual respect.

Hamer's farm closed when her health failed and management squabbled (cooperatives are TOUGH). But the mission resonated at a time when the movement was moving beyond ending segregation and focusing on the bigger, more vexing issue: POVERTY.

Complex, intractable issues of class and economics can often get ignored amid more passionate, symbolically loaded debates.

Movement leaders again and again drew focus back to basic issues of economic justice. Dr. King's late-life radicalism took the form of the Poor People's Campaign, which sought to force America to reckon with the ravages of poverty as it had the brutality of segregation.

Defying leaders who sought a narrower approach to civil rights, Dr. King launched a campaign to bring thousands of poor Americans to Washington, DC, to convene on the National Mall and put poverty on the doorstep of power. It was known as Resurrection City.

Dr. King was killed a month before the campaign began. Resurrection City was troubled from the start—disorganization and bad weather turned what organizers hoped would be a dramatic show of solidarity into a muddy pit. The Poor People's Campaign disbanded and pulled up stakes after six chaotic weeks.

Still, parts of that massive effort were hugely innovative. Like, for instance:

THE MULE TRAIN FROM MARKS was one of nine caravans organized to transport people to DC. The convoy from the tiny community of Marks, Mississippi, consisted of a lineup of covered wagons pulled by a team of mules, led by a pair called Bullet and Ava. Each wagon was painted with a message from the family inside:

Rumbling slowly along busy highways, trucks roaring past, the MULE TRAIN was a bracing vision of people cut off from modern American prosperity, a jolting reminder of class divisions and disparities.

In a questionnaire filled in during the caravan, participant Rose Kendrick wrote:

"Poor people do not get decent job and decent school. They do not get decent health care, do not get decent government and decent police. Poor people do not even get respect as human being. Congressmen, you have the job and you have the money. I WANT SOME OF IT SO I CAN LIVE TOO."

On the final miles to the National Mall, the clip-clopping of Bullet and Ava caused a traffic jam in DC.

It's a reminder that sometimes ACTIVISM IS ABOUT
MAKING A SCENE, producing a spectacle, creating an out-
of-the-ordinary event that engages masses of people (and
maybe even a mule or two).

KEEP FOCUS

Civil rights is often told as a story of war, a series of
battles planned by strategists, led by generals, fought by
foot soldiers.

That's how Jim Clark saw it.

A beefy Alabamian cattle rancher and army gunner in WWII,
Clark was sheriff of the rolling farmland around Selma.

Clark was a mean, hot-tempered military man. He stood guard at the county courthouse in full soldier's regalia.

When activists began a march from Selma to Montgomery on a voter registration drive, Clark met them with a posse of men on horseback and deputies in gas masks.

On the Edmund Pettus Bridge, he led the vicious charge.

The story of civil rights is filled with characters like Clark.

In Birmingham, Sheriff Bull Connor released dogs on children and turned fire hoses on peaceful protesters.

In Little Rock, Governor Orval Faubus (Orval Faubus!) dispatched troops to stop nine African American kids from attending high school.

A crowd of neighbors gathered to scream and shove and throw things.

So much anger, so much ignorance, so much hate.

All of which fueled groups like the Ku Klux Klan, with their RIDICULOUS GETUPS and burning crosses and hateful history of intimidation and murder. They met civil rights with TERRORISM.

Robert Chambliss joined the Klan at the age of twenty. A truck driver and army vet, he met with fellow Klansmen at a barbecue joint, where they worked each other up into frenzies over threats to the white race. When African Americans began buying homes in a white area of town, more than fifty dynamite sticks went off. People started calling Birmingham "Bombingham." Chambliss earned the nickname "Dynamite Bob."

On September 15, 1963, just two weeks after Dr. King made his "I Have a Dream" speech in Washington, fifteen sticks of dynamite went off under the steps of the Sixteenth Street Baptist Church. The blast blew out the church's stained-glass windows and destroyed a church basement and Sunday school classroom. The explosion killed four girls.

An investigation by the all-white Birmingham police force identified Dynamite Bob and four of his cronies as suspects, but no arrests were made. Chambliss remained free for fourteen years before finally facing charges.

A stained glass window recovered from the blast is now displayed across the street from the church, at the Birmingham Civil Rights Institute.

Not all the bad guys were so obvious. So-called Citizens' Councils were more like racist Rotary clubs, filled with more than sixty thousand Southerners who publicly condemned violence while fighting for "states' rights" and "racial integrity."

But that was just a front. NAACP field worker Medgar Evers was murdered in his front yard by a Council member named Byron De La Beckwith. The Council paid his legal fees.

And so it went, the movement met with lynchings and assassinations and bombings and beatings.

All the while, Southern politicians spoke of a cherished HERITAGE and the THREAT OF COMMUNISTS and OUTSIDE AGITATORS.

As a young man, George Wallace was by all accounts a moderate, fair-minded judge. Then, in his first run for governor of Alabama, he was trounced by an opponent who accepted help from the KKK and tried to banish the NAACP from Alabama.

Wallace won his next race, famously declaring, "segregation now, segregation tomorrow, and segregation forever." He went on to serve four terms as governor and make three runs for president, all the while railing against intellectuals and anarchists and "big-government elites."

He attacked the press, saying the media was "run and operated by left-wing liberals, Communist sympathizers, and members of ... Communist front organizations with HIGH-SOUNDING NAMES."

His rallies were raucous shindigs with country music and hollering crowds. Protesters hounded him with swastikas and signs: "If you liked Hitler, you'll love Wallace." He shouted them down with taunts and insults. The crowd ate it up.

Sound familiar?

THE LESSON: Just as the civil rights movement developed a powerful new playbook, opponents made a few useful discoveries themselves. They developed a brand of politics that drew power from fear of outsiders and elites, appealed to fabled past glory, and created excitement from insults, tantrums, and "straight talk."

More than anything, they appealed to the urge to RETALIATE, to get even. Still today, we fixate on our opponents and the way they are wrong. We think:

THIS IS WAR.
And we must win it.

And now here comes Dr. King, along with Bayard Rustin and James Lawson and Gandhi and Thoreau and Booker T. Washington.

"Let no man pull you so low
as to make you hate him."
— Booker T. Washington

Again and again, Dr. King FOCUSED THE MOVEMENT AWAY from the story of war and enemies and the vilification of bad guys. He sought reconciliation over victory, redemption over triumph.

THE ESSENTIAL LESSON: Keep your focus on the problem, not the people. Eyes on the prize. In other words,

FIGHT OPPRESSION, NOT OPPRESSORS.

Andrew Young was a close friend of Dr. King and a key civil rights figure. He went on to become a United Nations ambassador and mayor of Atlanta. Appearing at a civil rights panel in Los Angeles, Young says one guiding principle has guided all his work: FOCUS.

"When you call out your opponent's name you strengthen him. During the movement we didn't talk about Wallace. The more we focus on the conditions we want to change and the less we blame and fuss over the people responsible, the more we build support and create change."

In other words: Stop obsessing over the oppressors. Get to work exposing acts of oppression.

Or as historian Hasan Kwame Jeffries puts it:

"Don't reduce the causes of racial inequality to a few OUT-OF-CONTROL CRACKERS."

During the Selma voter-registration drive, Jim Clark cracked protesters over the head, shocked others with a cattle prod, and jailed more than thirty-four hundred people, many of them children.

After one tiresome day of beating and jailing protesters, Clark collapsed with chest pains.

It was raining the next day. A crowd of two hundred protesters knelt down on the wet steps outside Clark's office.

They carried signs: "Get well, Sheriff Clark!"

A minister led the group in prayer: "We are a nonviolent army and we wish no harm to anyone," he said. "We pray for the betterment of Sheriff Clark and for his family. We pray for him to recover. Bless him according to your divine will."

THAT'S IT, right there.

Could there be a more deserved target for collective outrage than Jim Clark? The man with the "NEVER" pin and the cattle prod?

And yet his opponents PRAYED for him. In a big public display.

Which was both spiritually heroic—and supersmart, tactically.

Rev. Richard Boone, the minister who led the prayer, insisted there was nothing cynical about it.

It made no difference to Clark—he remained defiant and unapologetic to his death. Still, the prayers from protesters made front pages across the country, sending a message far and wide.

This was a movement
about RECONCILIATION—
not revenge.

BE JOYOUS

Fighting oppression is critical business. Often the people doing it are earnest, judgy, and superserious. Ta-Nehisi Coates calls activists "professional scolds."

Then there's Bayard Rustin.

Dashing and Quaker, Rustin is best known for putting together the 1963 National March on Washington. He handled the bus routes and porta potties, crowd control and lunch boxes. (He banned mayo on the ham sandwiches for fear it'd go bad in the August heat.)

From choosing condiments to developing strategy, Rustin was there at pretty much every step of the civil rights story, advising and organizing and rabble-rousing.

Among the major civil rights leaders, he's characterized as the "master strategist and tactician."

And yet there was something even more impressive about Rustin: how he infused everything he did with a HUGE HEAP of JOIE DE VIVRE. A few years before his death, he was asked to describe his legacy:

"I HAD FUN."

Fun? Activism isn't supposed to be FUN.

And yet the movement was filled with dancing and singing and the highest of spirits. During the crisis in Birmingham, a local DJ got word out to teenagers that a mass arrest was planned by announcing on air,

"There's a PARTY IN THE PARK today. Bring your toothbrush because lunch will be served."

While kids faced fire hoses and dogs and hours in jail (that's what the toothbrushes were for), many found occasion for celebration. After firefighters turned their hoses on the crowd, kids turned up the next day in swimsuits. A few danced in the spray.

Bishop Calvin Woods was a preacher at East End Baptist
Church during the Birmingham protests. We get together on
his eighty-fourth birthday across the street from the city
square where the most violent clashes occurred. Looking back,
Bishop Woods remembers feeling intense joy and determination.

"People would scream and sing and pray—that's what kept us
motivated," he says. "We'd keep at it until we got happy. It
engendered inspiration and motivation."

It was infectious. "Some of those police got converted," he says. "They heard us saying and singing 'you gotta love everybody' and they couldn't help but get caught up.

They started singing along. The spirit grabbed 'em."

Calvin Woods

Mahalia Jackson

Music played a HUGE part in making the movement MOVE.
People made music at meetings and protests and sit-ins and
marches—events played out amid a wall-to-wall soundtrack of
FREEDOM SONGS: church hymns with rewritten lyrics, gospel
songs belted out in prison cells, and folk anthems imported
from the labor movement.

Bob Dylan

Robert Darden has spent much of his life studying the music of the movement, tracing melodies back to songs written by slave poets in cotton fields and forward to newer versions sung

by Egyptian students during the revolution in 2011. Freedom songs have always been about far more than boosting morale.

"These weren't just little ditties people sang to pass the time," he says. "There's something unique about this music, something deep and powerful."

WE SHALL OVERCOME

Mass meetings began and ended with song—and people kept it going as they walked home. "At the pivotal moment of African American history," Darden says, "they're singing maybe three-fourths of the time."

At the HIGHLANDER FOLK SCHOOL in Tennessee, song-leaders were trained to teach protesters and spread the songbook at events around the country. Darden: "Activists first learned how to take a punch—then, they learned the major songs of the movement."

Pete Seeger

Two obvious lessons:

1. MUSIC IS AS IMPORTANT AS ANYTHING IN THE ACTIVIST ARSENAL. It's not about "entertainment"— it's a resource to be cultivated and celebrated and included in any effective activist strategy.

"When the MOVEMENT is strong
the MUSIC is strong."
— Harry Belafonte

2. ACTIVISM IS A COMMUNITY ACTIVITY.

Music made a difference in civil rights because it was made in shared spaces, by and for people who GOT TOGETHER to march, protest, strategize, and sing.

SUPPORT PLANNED PARENTHOOD

Virtual canvassing and online activism are well and good, but if the civil rights movement teaches us nothing else, it's the power of ACTUAL REAL-LIFE COMMUNITY.

When in doubt, gather people together.

You know who understood the power of music and a good get-together? BAYARD RUSTIN.

He was that rarest of people: the guy you'd want to plan the party and the guy you'd want AT the party. His life story offers two or three or seven vital lessons in activism and life.

Growing up in rural Pennsylvania, Bayard played high school football. He was a fierce tackler with a peculiar habit: After flattening an opponent, he'd recite a choice stanza of Elizabethan poetry. (I loved that story even more when I heard recordings of Rustin's precise upper-crust elocution—he talked like Cary Grant!)

He was kicked out of college for organizing a student strike. He moved to Harlem, joined and then quit the Communist Party, and spent three years in a federal penitentiary as a conscientious objector during WWII. While he was behind bars, he desegregated the mess hall and learned to play the lute.

THE LUTE!

Later, he released an album of Elizabethan songs and Negro spirituals.

Not long after leaving jail,
he joined a group of Quakers
testing federal antisegregation laws on interstate buses. He
was sentenced to twenty-two days on a chain gang. He wrote
about the horrendous conditions for a New York paper.

And oh yeah: He never made a secret of being gay. That made him a favorite target of civil rights foes. Strom Thurmond called him a "deviant" on the floor of Congress.

Bayard took it as a badge of honor. A friend said Bayard "never knew there was a closet to go into."

Bayard traveled to India to work with Gandhi's movement. (Biographer Jervis Anderson called Bayard "a leading member of the RADICAL JET SET.")

When he got back to the States, he went to Montgomery to help with the bus boycott.

It was a terrifying time. MLK's house had been bombed and the city was threatening to arrest a hundred boycott organizers.

But Bayard found a way to elevate and enliven the whole shebang.

It was Bayard, along with Quaker reverend Glenn Smiley, who schooled MLK in the Gandhian philosophy of nonviolence, convincing the twenty-seven-year-old preacher to get rid of his guns and embrace nonviolence not just as a tactic but as a way of life.

When rumors spread about the police dragnet, Bayard had an idea.

Rather than sitting at home waiting for police to arrive, Bayard urged the boycott leaders to head down to the sheriff's office in their Sunday best.

"You looking for me?" E. D. Nixon said, marching up to the police station. "Well, HERE I AM."

Others joined, cheering as the organizers gave themselves up to the police and roaring even louder after they were released on bail. It turned into a party.

It got so loud that the sheriff stepped out and hollered, "This ain't no vaudeville show!"

That was Bayard. **Where others saw a threat, he saw a party.**

"He was all about creativity and turning nonviolent philosophy into joyful force."

That's Walter Naegle, Bayard's companion for the last ten years of his life. In 2013, Walter accepted the Presidential Medal of Freedom in Bayard's memory from President Obama. We eat lunch one summer afternoon at a coffee shop in Chelsea.

He talked about meeting Bayard in Times Square in the late seventies, about their trips to Europe and Africa to work on peace initiatives, and about Bayard's remarkable ability to turn serious work into the happiest of experiences.

"If he wasn't having fun, he wouldn't do it. It was dangerous work and it involved constant risks, but he enjoyed it. He knew how to be militant, but he was also just a lot of fun to be around."

The lesson is clear enough:

BRING THE JOY.

Suffering and sacrifice may be transformative, but at a certain point PAIN IS NO GOOD TO ANYBODY.

The work of social justice can be dire and daunting, but the mood doesn't have to be.

CONCLUSION

"If there is NO STRUGGLE there is NO PROGRESS. Those who profess to favor FREEDOM and yet deprecate AGITATION are men who want CROPS without PLOWING UP THE GROUND, they want RAIN without THUNDER and lightning. They want the OCEAN without the AWFUL ROAR of its many waters."

— Frederick Douglass

Dr. King's tomb is mounted on a platform in a shallow fountain in downtown Atlanta. He's laid next to his wife, Coretta, at the King Center on Auburn Avenue, a block away from his childhood home and Ebenezer Church, where his father preached.

Rows of schoolbuses rumble nearby. A PA system plays bad inspirational melodies and random facts: "Did you know that Dr. King drove a 1957 Chevrolet Impala?" (I did not.)

Across the way is a National Park museum filled with mementos and exhibits reminding us to "remember the dream" and "stand up for equality."

Got it. It's all very educational and interesting.

Then, tucked in a glass cabinet of a small upstairs gallery, something hits home.

His boots.

Dr. King walked fifty miles from Selma to Montgomery in these shoes. It looks like you could slip them on yourself and start walking.

As far as mementos go, Dr. King's Nobel medal is fine—but the boots give me the SHIVERS.

All of a sudden, I get a flash of ENERGY and DARING and RADICALISM.

Bodies in space, eyes on the prize, a determined coalition kicking the legs out from under a seemingly unmovable system…

In Montgomery a few days later I visit the offices of a young lawyer named Evan Milligan. He works for the Equal Justice Initiative, which deals with mass incarceration, juvenile justice, and civil rights.

He's not a fan of the way the movement is portrayed at museums like the King Center.

"The sanitized presentation of the civil rights movement lets too many people OFF THE HOOK. You get to say, there was Rosa Parks and there was the 'I Have a Dream' speech and the Civil Rights Act, and then you're done. We were bad and blind but now we're all good. Now we have the NBA and the NFL and Budweiser and it's all fine."

The reality is NOT FINE.

The movement may have put an end to Jim Crow, but schools are still segregated,

voting rights are still suppressed,

and the combination of criminal injustice and mass incarceration has become **a new form of oppression and slavery.**

The fact is, segregationists never gave up their fight. Many still believe in the Lost Cause, the idea that the slaveholding South was an antebellum Eden that was viciously invaded by Northern aggressors.

They pass this belief down to their kids, where it gets mixed up with familial love and hardens into deep tribal identities.

"The people who fought for the Confederacy and who fought against integration are still with us," says Milligan. "They hung on—they maintained their ideology and their power."

Which brings us back to the question I started with, standing on the street back in Memphis . . .

HOW DO WE GO ON?

The movement has suggestions. It offers hard-won wisdom and advice:

Put your **BODY** in it.

Get comfortable with

DISRUPTION.

Understand the value of **SUFFERING.**

Focus on

OPPRESSION,

Not oppressors.

REJECT *violence.*

Get ORGANIZED.

Bring JOY.

Stop waiting for LEADERS.

Summon SOUL FORCE.

And perhaps most importantly, COME TO TERMS with the scope and scale and history of the struggle.

The movement toward justice and equality and equity and integration and mutuality—toward Dr. King's BELOVED COMMUNITY—is ongoing and unfinished and did not, and sadly will not, end in a happily-ever-after VICTORY PARTY where we celebrate a new law or a new president.

This story does not end with us easing back and congratulating one another.

But oh boy—doesn't that sound EXHAUSTING?

Especially in a time of high alert and intense polarization, when all manner of civil liberties and basic rights are under attack. We feel crazy and cynical and paralyzed. It feels as if we're fast approaching SYSTEM BREAKDOWN. We're buffeted by wave after wave of OUTRAGE. We lose faith and sleep and friends.

On this, the movement is clear. Like the song says:

"Ain't gonna let nobody turn me around. Gonna keep on walking. Keep on talking. Marching on to FREEDOMLAND."

As we march, we must remember:

Outrage isn't activism.

The people on the front lines of civil rights had a LOT TO BE OUTRAGED ABOUT. But they channeled all that upset into action. They PRAYED WITH THEIR FEET.

And that didn't always mean MARCHING. Joan Trumpauer Mulholland, whose head was doused with sugar and who spent weeks in a Mississippi penitentiary, is adamant about the importance of people who do the hard, everyday background work.

"Frontline people are good—but there have to be people driving cars, answering phones, doing paperwork. You can't have a successful movement without both groups."

 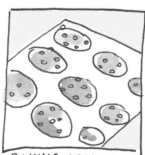 

STUFFIN' ENVELOPES   BAKING COOKIES   "CRAFTIVISM"

Georgia Gilmore was a single mother of six when the Montgomery bus boycott began. Gruff and outspoken, she was fired from a kitchen job after her boss found out she was helping the movement. She kept right on feeding people, making sandwiches to hand out at rallies and mass meetings.

Soon her cramped kitchen became a center of the action, and Gilmore and a group of friends were serving full chicken dinners at home and delivering pies and cakes and funneling all the proceeds back to the movement. To avoid detection by city officials, they called themselves THE CLUB FROM NOWHERE, and it became the single biggest financial backer of the boycott.

Not bad for a laid-off cook.

WE FACE AN UNCERTAIN FUTURE.

We have reasons to be afraid. Even beyond civil rights—
from asylum for refugees to the protection of the environment
to women's health—fundamental values are under attack.

And at a certain point we've all got to stop, step back, disengage from the panic of the moment, and ask ourselves: What can I do?

It's great to sign petitions, show up for town halls and protests, and make calls to members of Congress. But the best actions are those uniquely suited to those who do them.

As Joanne Bland asked those boys on the bridge at Selma: What's your piece of the puzzle?

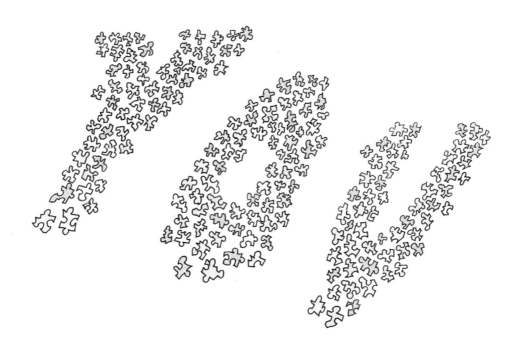

Because if you wonder what you would've done if you were alive during the civil rights movement, remember one thing:

You ARE.

Reading List

For further reading and watching:

Civil Rights History from the Ground Up, edited by Emilye Crosby (University of Georgia Press, 2011). Academic but not off-putting roundup of contemporary scholarship, challenging conventional wisdom and correcting omissions and falsehoods. Excellent entry on the Mule Train from Marks, Mississippi, to Washington, D.C.

Eyes on the Prize (1987–1990). Essential fourteen-part PBS documentary on the history of the movement from 1950s to 1980s, including tons of newsreel footage and commentary from movement veterans.

Just Mercy by Bryan Stevenson (Spiegel & Grau, 2014). The justifiably praised first-person account of an idealistic young lawyer and a corrupt, deeply racist criminal justice system. A bracing picture of the new realities of the civil rights struggle.

George Wallace: Settin' the Woods on Fire (2000). This documentary of the segregationist governor offers a scarily relevant tutorial on the politics of rage.

March by John Lewis and Andrew Aydin, illustrated by Nate Powell (Top Shelf Productions, 2013). Gorgeous three-volume comic centering on Lewis's role in struggle. Also graphic and also great: *Martin Luther King and the Montgomery Story* by Alfred Hassler and Benton Resnik (Fellowship of Reconciliation), a sixteen-page comic published in 1957 used as a training guide for activists; and *We Had Sneakers, They Had Guns* (Syracuse University Press, 2009), a book of on-the-scene illustrations by Tracy Sugarman.

Nothing but Love in God's Water: Volume 1 by Robert Darden (Pennsylvania Sate University Press, 2014). Exhaustive, exhilarating chronology of music of the movement, tracing its roots from slave songs to protest music of today.

Parting the Waters: America in the King Years, 1954-63 by Taylor Branch (Simon & Schuster, 1988). This history of Martin Luther King Jr. and the civil rights movement is exhaustive, novelistic, and epic. There are also two other volumes in this trilogy, *Pillar of Fire* (1998) and *At Canaan's Edge* (2006) that take the story up to 1968.

Strategies for Freedom by Bayard Rustin (Columbia University Press, 1976). Concise and clear-headed, Rustin's argument for the value of nonviolence and pragmatic negotiations resonates today. Also check out the documentary *Brother Outsider: The Life of Bayard Rustin* (2003) for a look at the pioneering, joyful leader.

Stride toward Freedom (Harper & Row, 1958) and *Where Do We Go from Here: Chaos or Community?* (Beacon Press, 1967) by Martin Luther King Jr. Written at the end of the Montgomery bus boycott and a year before his death, respectively, these bookend manifestos are essential (and pleasurable) reading.

The New Jim Crow by Michelle Alexander (New Press, 2010). Enlightening, infuriating look at mass incarceration, the War on Drugs, and the modern face of systematic racism.

This Is an Uprising by Mark Engler and Paul Engler (Nation Books, 2016). Incisive, expansive survey of direct action and civil disobedience with emphasis on how civil rights inspired movements from Occupy to Black Lives Matter.

This Little Light of Mine: The Life of Fannie Lou Hamer by Kay Mills (University Press of Kentucky, 1993). Epic biography of the too-often overlooked grassroots leader.

We Shall Not Be Moved by M. J. O'Brien (University Press of Mississippi, 2013). Minute-by-minute account of the famed Woolworth's sit-in with backstories of all participants including Joan Trumpauer Mulholland.

Editor: David Cashion
Designer: Liam Flanagan
Production Manager: Kathleen Gaffney

Library of Congress Control Number: 2018931067

ISBN: 978-1-4197-3235-5
eISBN: 978-1-68335-346-1

Printed and bound in China
10 9 8 7 6 5 4 3 2 1

Abrams books are available at special discounts when
purchased in quantity for premiums and promotions as
well as fundraising or educational use. Special editions
can also be created to specification. For details, contact
specialsales@abramsbooks.com or the address below.

ABRAMS The Art of Books
195 Broadway, New York, NY 10007
abramsbooks.com